Before we get started...

This book is dedicated to Christopher and Anthony Bowman. Babysitting you both was one of the first jobs I ever had, and taught me valuable lessons on responsibility, money, and choices. You both went from little crying, light skinned, pooping machines to handsome, bright men who I'm confident are going to do great things one day. You both inspire me, and give me grey hair.

Congratulations, you've made join the ranks of some of the world's most revolutionary and innovative individuals by deciding to become an entrepreneur. Entrepreneurship is what our culture and the entire world is built on. The places you eat, the things you buy, the technology you use, all started out as an idea in someone's head. The world needs entrepreneurs and the innovation they bring to the table. When you read this book, be excited for the possibilities that come with becoming an entrepreneur. You will evolve into a great professional with a great business to match, and an even better human being. Make sure you use the sheets I provided at the end of the book to keep track of your progress.

My Story

Have you just been walking around, living life one day, and you just stop and think, "I want more. I can be more." I had just graduated college and came back home excited about what was in store for me. I finally had my golden ticket to adulthood and could, quite literally, do what I wanted! Whoo hoo! But I never expected for things to take a turn the way that they did. Finding a job after school was an incredibly, miserable and degrading process for me. I would fill out thousands of applications until I couldn't write or see straight. Answering the same questions over and over, finding different ways to say, "Give me a job dammit! I'm trying to be an adult!" I would get calls to come in for interviews and feel like a fool for even showing up. I'd feel like every time I opened my mouth I was begging them for a chance, and they shut me down every time.

Sidebar: Don't you just love how when you apply to entry level jobs now they ask that you have 8,000 years of experience? That to me is one of the stupidest things that a job could require for an entry level job. Clearly if I'm applying for this position I don't have any experience, and money. It's like they are too lazy to train you so they're just like, "ugh, just come in knowing how to do everything so that we don't have to do anything."

So because I was not able to find a job, I slipped into what I like to refer to as, "pre-depression." I was feeling terrible! I had spent all this time in college, to graduate and not even be able to find a job? How pathetic of me! But one day, I came up with the crazy idea of starting a blog. Nothing major, just something to keep my mind and my hands busy. I had always wanted to have my own blog because I loved to write and I wanted a voice for myself. I had lived my young life plagued by insecurities and not so wise decisions, I just felt like it was time to open my mind and my mouth. I had no clue that this would become a business for me.

To me, I think that's how most businesses start. It's just one person who is really passionate about something, or someone looking to change something in their life, or in their community, and then BOOM, it takes off! So Exquisite Charleston saved me from slipping into, what could have been, a very bad time for me...It saved me! It redeemed my faith in myself and my abilities, but also in my community.

What started off as a music blog, evolved quickly into a now, online and seasonal print magazine. In addition to the magazine, I also have a mobile app, a scholarship fund for students looking to pursue degrees in the Media, Communications, and Journalism industries, and a creative sector, called Profound Solutions. With Profound Solutions, the skills I have learned and applied to my business, I offer to other businesses like social media management, marketing consulting, business coaching, graphic design, event coordination, just to name a few. My business has definitely come a long way in the almost 5 years that's it's been in existence. So many lessons learned, so many relationships built, so much growth from myself and the brand as well. If I've learned anything about entrepreneurship, it's definitely that you will NEVER have it all figured out. The most seasoned of business owners still learn new things to expand daily.

    Being a dope entrepreneur is more about fighting the good fight for change, while keeping an open mind towards everything that will come your way. You have to be willing to accept a challenge, and get back up no matter how many times you fail or stumble. It's about doing what you love and inspiring others to do the same. You never initially start out like that, and clearly I didn't, but hopefully this book will mold you to be the best version of yourself, professionally and personally. Buckle your seat belts, this going to be yet another bumpy ride!

Paperwork, Legal Stuff and other boring stuff you need to do

Now before we do anything, unfortunately I have to inform you of the boring, and technical side of entrepreneurship. I call it boring stuff because...well it is boring! But knowing all of this information, and having some general understanding of it will protect you, and your business, in the long run. Me personally, I didn't learn about much of this until a year and a half after I had already started my business. I never knew I needed a business license, never understood what copyrights and trademarks were. See...aren't you lucky to have me to help you? Let's get started.

Your Name

So let me tell you the story of how I got the name of my business. I'd always listen to music every day when I'd walk home from school, various different genres, and different artists. There was this one song that somehow, some way found its way onto my iPod and it was by Lil Wayne called, "So Exquisite." I remember listening to it, and now that I think about it I don't remember a damn thing he said on the song, I just liked how the word "exquisite" sounded every time they said it on the chorus, so the word just kind of stuck with me.

I went home and looked up the word exquisite and a synonym for it is excellent. I liked the word excellent because when I was in school, my teachers always described me as an "excellent student." So I added the word "so" in front of it because I felt like I was "so excellent!" Not long after I added Charleston onto it because Charleston is where I grew up and it's all I've ever known. The history, the culture, and the people are so diverse and the city itself has become such a melting pot of everything. So when you put all those words together, So Exquisite Charleston is excellent diversity. Mind blown.

When I first had my mind set on a name for my business, before I told my friends, before I told my family, before I made anything final, I Googled it. Just for fun really, but then I found at least 3 other businesses with basically the same name. I'd suggest you do the same thing before you set anything in stone. Creativity is always the key when coming up with a good name for your business. You want something that is impressionable and easy to remember. Once you know what you want to call your business, now you'll need to protect that name. There are a few ways you can do that:

- Entity name: This is protects you at a state level, and is basically how the states identifies your business. Depending on your states, your business structure, and location, you may be required to register a legal entity name.
- Trademark: protects your business name, goods, and services at a federal level. It prevents others in the same industry in America from using your name.
- Doing Business as (DBA) name: This is only required if your business has a DBA, and that varies by states. A DBA is a trade name, or assumed name, for your business, which allows you to operate under a different identity.
- Domain name: This is the name of your business' website and by registering your domain, no one else can use it as long as you own it, which is essentially for protecting your brand presence online.

Structure Your Business

Once you've gotten your name registered, then it's time to figure out how you would like for your business to be structure. The business structure that you choose for your business influences every aspect of your business from your day-to-day operations, taxes, and how much of your personal assets are at risk. The structure that you choose is dependent on how many people you decide to go into business with:

Sole Proprietorship: one individual or married couple that are in business alone. They are the most common business structure and are simplest to form and operate. You pay fewer taxes, fewer legal controls, flexibility on management, but you as the sole owner are personally liable for all debts of the business.

- <u>Documents needed:</u> None.

General Partnership: 2 or more people who each contribute money, labor and skill to the business. They each share the profits and losses of the business, manage, and are each personally and equally liable for the debts of the partnership. This is a good option for businesses with multiple owners who want to test their business idea before forming a more formal business. There are two common types of partnerships: Limited partnerships (LP), where only one general partner has unlimited liability and all others have limited liability, and Limited Liability Partnerships (LLP).

- <u>Documents needed to file:</u> For a LP and LLP, you'll need to file a Certificate of Limited Partnership, or Certificate of Limited Liability Partnership, and the Limited Partnership Agreement, or Limited Liability Partnership Agreement. The Certificate or LP describes the basics of your partnership, and notifies the state of your existence. Just basic information on your business. The LP Agreement is an internally binding document between all of the partners that defines how the business decisions get made, each person's duties, powers, and responsibilities. This isn't always required but it's good to have it to protect yourself and the business.

Limited Liability Corporation (LLC): formed by one or more people, or entities, through a special written agreement. This agreement details the organization of the LLC, management for the business, assigned interests, and distribution of profits and losses. These structures protect you from personal liability in most instances; your personal assets won't be at risk in case the LLC faces lawsuits or bankruptcy. Profits and losses can get passed through your personal income without faces corporate taxes. However, members of an LLC are considered self-employed and must pay self-employment tax contributions towards Medicare and Social Security.

- **Documents needed to file:** For a LLC, you'll need to file your Articles of Organization, and the LLC Operating agreement. The Articles of Organization is a document that describes the basics of your LLC and includes information such as your company name, registered agent, address, and member names. The LLC Operating Agreement describes the structure of your company's financial and functional decisions. It defines how key business decisions are made, as well as each member's duties, powers, and responsibilities. Some states don't require this, but it's recommended to protect yourself and the business.

Corporation: a more complex business structure that has certain rights, privileges, and liabilities beyond those of an individual. Corporations may yield tax or financial benefits, but these can be offset by other considerations, such as increased licensing fees or decreased personal control. Nonprofit Corporation is an entity that runs to further an ideal or goal rather than make a profit. These organizations are tax exempt and owners are not personally liable, but corporate profits can't be distributed.

- **Documents needed to file:** For any corporation, you'll need to file the Articles of Incorporation, or a Certificate of Incorporation, and Bylaws or Resolutions, for nonprofits. The Articles of

Incorporation is a legal document that lays out the basic outline of your business, like the Articles of Organization for an LLC; it includes basic essential information about your business. Your Bylaws are the internal governance documents of a corporation. They define how key business decisions are made, as well as officer and shareholders' duties, powers, and responsibilities. Some states don't require this, but it's recommended to protect yourself and the business.

Now once you've decided how you want to structure your business, you'll then need to register with the state where you plan to conduct your business. If you plan on doing business in more than one state, you'll need to file for foreign qualification in other states where your business will be active. The state where you formed your business will consider your business to be domestic there, but in other states it's considered foreign. You'll also be required to pay taxes and annual fees in your state of formation and all the states you do business in. Some states are with the times and actually let you register all this stuff online, while some make you go through the annoying process of sending in paper applications.

Keep in mind that there are fees that come along with registering your business, depending on the structure, but again those fees vary based on the state you are in.

When you are registering your business, you'll have to get a registered agent, which is just someone they send official papers and legal documents to. This can be yourself or you can use a registered agent service if you don't want to.

Tax ID Numbers

Now I've been talking about taxes for the past few sections, but in order to actually file your taxes your business needs an EIN number! EIN stands for employee identification number, and it basically allows you to pay federal taxes, hire employees, open a bank account, and apply for business licenses and permits. It's free to get and you'll definitely need it if you plan to pay employees, file tax returns, and many other things. It's free to apply for on the IRS' website and you should do it right after you register your business.

You'll also need to get a state tax ID number in order to pay state taxes. The process is the same as getting an EIN with the IRS, but it can vary by state and you'd have to check with your state government for specific steps.

Business Licenses and Permits

Now while I can sit here and tell you how rewarding and awesome being an entrepreneur is...well wait, that's the point of this book so technically I will. It's important to also remember that with running a business there are also legal parts that need to be taken care of, and kept up with, in order to stay in business. Would it suck if you started doing business and then a few months later you got shut down for not having the proper permits or licenses? Yeah it would suck big time so make sure you read this part if you don't pay attention to anything else I tell you.

This part is usually where many people get confused or tend to worry most. I know for me, I never even knew I needed a business license, and didn't get one until almost a year and a half after I had already started my business. So don't stress yourself out too bad about these things if you don't have them yet. For those who may run a home based it's a little easier to fly under the radar without these versus those who may be looking to open a store front. Nonetheless, its best to get these bad boys in the beginning rather than wait until it's too late.

- *Business License:* permits issued by the government that allows a business to be conducted within that certain government's geographical jurisdiction.

- *Fire Department Permit:* needed if your business uses any flammable materials, or if your premises will be open to the public. In most cities, you need it before you can actually open your business, and sometimes periodic inspections are done to make sure your business meets safety regulations.
- *Air and Water Pollution Control Permit:* If you burn any materials, discharge anything into the sewers or waterways, or use products that produce gas, even paint sprayers, you will need this permit.
- *Sign Permit:* Some cities have sign ordinances that restrict the size, location, lighting, and the type of sign you can use outside of your business.
- *County Permits:* If your business lies outside of a city or town's jurisdiction, you may need to have one of these in order to conduct business.
- *State Licenses:* In some states, people with certain occupations are required to have permits. Some examples include plumbers, building contractors, collection agents, auto mechanics, barbers, insurance agents, etc.
- *Federal Licenses:* few types of businesses require federal licensing, but The Federal Trade Commission can confirm which ones do and don't.

- *Sales Tax License:* These sometimes go by a "certificate of resale," "seller's permit," or "certificate of authority." Any home-based business selling taxable goods and services must pay sales taxes on what it sells. Sales taxes vary by state, and some states consider it a criminal offense to conduct a sale without one.
- *Health Department Permits:* If you plan to sell food, either directly to customers in a restaurant or as a wholesaler to other retailers, you'll need this permit.

Copyrights and Trademarks

Copyrights and trademarks were one of the more tricky things to understand and apply for when I first got started. For a while I initially thought of both of them to be the same thing, but they are actually not and many don't know that. While they are similar in their protection, they both protect different things.

A copyright is the exclusive right to reproduce, publish, or sell, your work of authorship. So really only things that are tangible or physical can be copyrighted, not things like ideas or concepts, but if they are inside of a book then they can be. A trademark is specifically for a business or brand, and protects words and symbols that represent it, like a logo and slogan.

For example if you create a new type of car, you can trademark the logo of your company and the name, but copyright the actual car. When you want to copyright or trademark anything, I'd recommend searching to make sure someone already hasn't beaten you to the punch.

You can search copyrights on this website:
http://cocatalog.loc.gov/cgi-bin/Pwebrecon.cgi?DB=local&PAGE=First

You can search trademarks on this website:
http://tmsearch.uspto.gov/bin/gate.exe?f=tess&state=4803:tr2yvk.1.1

Once you've searched to make sure someone else hasn't copyrighted or trademarked your brand or product, now it's time to apply. Keep in mind, there are fees associated with applying for both and they can add up a bit. Copyrights are cheaper, and usually, depending on if you have numerous things to copyright or not, or if you do it online or mail in an application, it can cost you as much as $50. You can apply for a copyright online at https://www.copyright.gov/ and print out forms there also if you prefer to mail everything in. Trademarks can usually run you anywhere from $275-$325, depending on the kind of application you do. Each of those applications are explained here for trademarks: https://www.uspto.gov/

Keep in mind; you don't have to do these before opening your business. A lot of businesses don't get these until way after they've already opened their doors. But if you prefer to do it before, then there is no harm in doing it.

Important Stuff To Read Ahead

Now that we've got all of the boring stuff out of the way, allow me to drop some knowledge on you.

I'm in no way an entrepreneurship guru, and there honestly is no such thing as one. As I've said multiple times, and will say, no one has it all figured out, and no one will ever figure it out. A lot of what most seasoned entrepreneurs know is really based on trial and error, and honey, I've made a lot errors.

What may work for some, may not work for all. The following are rules for being an entrepreneur, and becoming a dope entrepreneur, that I have learned on my journey.

Being a Professional and Professionalism

Remember before when I mentioned how I became a new person when I started a business? I grew from a shy young girl, to a confident business woman! Much of that growth came with having to take on this new persona as a professional when conducting business and representing your brand. Apart of being a professional, is knowing how to conduct yourself like one, and doing that is called professionalism. When most people think of professionalism they think of fancy suits, briefcases, good customer service, and carrying yourself in a very "I mean business," type of style.

Now from what I've learned, most professionals don't fit this stereotype, and neither will you. There are particular standards of professionalism that's universal for any entrepreneur or business, but everybody has their own interpretations of them and some people just don't practice them. The professional conduct and professionalism of you can either make or break your business' reputation. For example, not showing up to meetings on time or being rude to customers when they call your establishment. Even how you deal with that criticism, customer complaints, or anything in your professional setting can create a reputation for you. What kind of reputation do you want for yourself and your business? Do you want to be someone known as a slacker who provides poor customer service to clients, and is always late to meetings and functions? Or would you rather be someone who is known for excellent and quick service, quality products, and great communication? No one is saying you have to become a whole new person, but you want to be the type of professional that people want to work with, and push those qualities that make people want to work with you, through your business so that people will want to patronize your business. A great way to think about it is to just treat others how you would want them to treat you.

Here are some things to keep in mind when molding your professional conduct. If you can master these, then you get an A+ in Professionalism:

- *Appearance:* A professional is neat in person! I'd like to think that all human beings would be neat anytime they walk out of their door, but atlas that is not always the case. Definitely any time you walk out of your door, in the name of your business, you want to make sure that you are dressed appropriately for where ever you may be headed. Now this doesn't mean you always have to have on a suit and tie, or a formal dress, but dress appropriate for you. If you are a painter, then clearly a suit and tie is not going to be your everyday wear, or if you are a teacher, or a PR consultant, or a chef, am I making my point? Your appearance will vary based on your business and the occasion. Just make sure you come with your hair and take a shower at least!

- *Demeanor:* Your demeanor is your outward behavior. Any entrepreneur, in my opinion, should always appear confident and polite at all times. Why would anyone want to talk to someone who looks mean or comes off to cocky? That can create an unpleasant experience, which could lead to a bad reputation for you. Remember the saying, fake it till you make it? Well, even if you are having the worst day ever, your demeanor should still be positive.
- *Reliability:* No one wants to do business with someone they can't rely on. As a professional you are always counted on to get the job done for your peers, your customers, and your community.
- *Competence:* Later on, I'll talk about the importance of doing research. Good professionalism is always having knowledge of your industry, your products, and your services. People can respect a person that knows what they are talking about and can answer all their questions. How can you trust a business or professional that doesn't know anything?

- *Ethics:* Depending on the industry you are in, you may or may not have a strict code of ethics for your field. Either way, you should display ethical behavior at all times. It's just common sense if you ask me!
- *Maintaining Your Poise:* You are an entrepreneur, which means you are the boss and have to make all the bad decisions. Good professionalism is being able to handle that pressure and stress of difficult choices and decisions and still conduct yourself calmly and politely while resolving the issue at hand.
- *Phone Etiquette:* I can recall many times calling an establishment and having someone answer in a rude way, or seemed to be in a rush to get me off of the phone. You never know who is on the other end of the phone sometimes, so conduct yourself as if you were talking to the person face to face.
- *Written Correspondence:* Have you ever been intimidated by an email? Trust me, I've been there! Your polite demeanor and other positive qualities should shine in person and through written correspondence also. There is no need for big words, long drawn out statements. Be direct, be clear, and be polite.
- *Organizational Skills:* No one likes a messy person in general, and when you are unorganized

and messy when in business, it can send a different message than it would in a casual setting.
- *Accountability:* Professionals are accountable for their actions at all times! If you make a mistake, own up to it and try to fix it. Placing blame, or arguing, or anything that doesn't involve resolving the issue is never good professionalism.

Marketing vs. Branding

If I had to choose, branding and marketing would both be my favorite things about being an entrepreneur. I've always considered myself to be a creative individual, and branding and marketing really have allowed me to flex those muscles as I pleased. Many entrepreneurs I've encountered always seemed to use these two words interchangeably as if they are the same, when really they both are different, but work together for the sake of the business. Before you start cramming out a marketing strategy, you need to build your foundation first. You can't market a business if it has no face, and that face of the business is your logo.

Everything starts with the logo! Your logo establishes your color scheme for your business as well, which you incorporate into your branding and marketing. The colors of my logo are blue and white, so most of my marketing you see the blue and white predominately, and maybe a bit of gray and a dash of black every now and then. How you brand your business is just as important as all of the other parts of your business. This is what draws people into your business and makes them loyal. Your marketing is the avenue you use to do that, like through radio advertisements, television commercials, social media advertising, events, flyers, brochures, emails, I could really go on and on with the different types of marketing and it would make your head spin. A marketing strategy is how you promote your branding and your business, and if done right, it convinces you to shop or do business with a company; the branding keeps you interested.

    Keep in mind that while there are tons of ways you can market to people, there may only be a few ways that apply to your target audience. Your target audience is who you are selling to and/or who you want to buy your products. For example, you may sell a denture cream; your target audience would be people who wear dentures. People who wear those may be older and not know how to work a computer, or be on social media, so you'd tailor your marketing strategy to more traditional avenues like television and radio for example. Make sense? But of course when coming up with a marketing strategy and getting to know your target audience, you want to do research and not just go based off of assumptions.

To create a strong and kick-ass brand, follow these steps:

- Create a brilliant vision for your business and make a promise to your customers and deliver on that promise.
- Provide your audience with products and services that are relevant to them and their needs.
- Have a clear target audience and created a marketing strategy to appeal to them.
- Integrate your brand into every aspect of your business. For example, how you answer the phone, your email signature, how you conduct business with other organizations and customers.
- Develop a tagline for your business that leaves a lasting impression on all those who encounter it
- Design templates and brand standards that capture the essence of your brand and echo through all aspects of your business.

No More School!

For so long we've been taught that life goes like this: be born, be a kid, go to school, go to college, get a job, have a family, and then die. But society has come so far in the past 5-10 years that this traditional path we are trained to go down, is now least popular. I get so many people that come up to me about wanting to do something different with their lives, wanting a change, and wanting to break away from tradition, and they see entrepreneurship as the way for them to do that. One question I get all the time is, "do I have to go back to college and get a degree in business in order to become an entrepreneur." While 20 years ago, the answer to that may have been yes, the answer now is definitely "no" now. You look at people like Oprah and Steve Jobs and many others, and their backgrounds of being college and high school drop outs, and look at them now, it's not secret as to why people are passing up on student loan debt and starting a business cold turkey.

      Besides the success stories of other entrepreneurs who don't have business degrees, a lot of people see the cost of going to college as money that could be put into starting their business, along with the time that goes into. Now I'm saying all this, not to encourage you NOT to get a business degree, but just to show you that it is possible to be successful without it. There are many people who start their businesses and go back to school eventually to get their business degree. Having a degree may not be necessary but it does add credibility to you when approaching banks and institutions for loans, grants, or investments. There tons of knowledge to be gained from getting a business degree, even though you may know some of it, it still wouldn't hinder you in any way to learn more and expand your skill set.

You Don't Need Money...Right Away

I started my business with no money. Just a dream and incredible will power. That's how businesses start for many people, and that's what keeps them going. So essentially, no you don't need a ton of money or any money to start a business. But there are things to consider like your licenses or permits that you may need before opening your doors, or any equipment you may need as well. But again that all depends on what kind of business you seek to have. Someone opening a restaurant may need a small business loan to get started, versus someone who just wants to be a PR consultant or business coach. And if money is your concern when it comes to getting started, it's okay to start small and grow.

For example, if you want to open a restaurant, but don't have the money to do it and can't get a loan from the banks, why not start off as a mobile catering business? Less initial expenses, you can start bringing revenue to save up for expansion, grow the support and customer base, and then when you move to a store front your business grows even more. It pays off in the long run to just take baby steps in the beginning.

Be Passionate or Nothing At All

Now while I still work a full time job, in addition to be an entrepreneur, I've had the pleasure of meeting people who are lucky enough to be running their business full time. Good. GOOD FOR THEM! But what is so strange to me is how they start their business, and then just treat it like it's another job. They put in all this time and energy, just for it to be another job to them. Think about it, what keeps you at your job? MONEY AND BILLS. These people start their businesses just for money. They aren't passionate about what they are doing, who they are servicing, and how it affects anything, and that's disturbing to me. I really don't think they realize that they are doing it either because we've become so accustomed to an employee mindset, that we don't know how to shake it, even when we aren't the employee anymore.

You can't be a successful entrepreneur if you aren't passionate about what you are doing, otherwise you are just in it for the money and honey, the money is not guaranteed to come all the time. Most businesses don't see a real profit until maybe 2-3 years in. Yeah, you may be making money right now, but is that money enough for the business to sustain itself and for you to live off of? So if the money is not coming in like you want or dreamed for it to, then what's keeping you motivated? What's gonna make you not just want to give up after a few weeks of no profit? Employees care about the money, entrepreneurs care about the future. Of course you want to make money by having a business, but that can't be your sole reason for all of this work, all of this time, all of this...EVERYTHING! You have to want more!

Talk to Yourself Sometimes

For a lot of us who go into business by ourselves, you are your most trusted adviser and responsible for making all of the decisions for your business. Responsibility like this can be stressful and overwhelming for many people. So don't fret, you aren't weak or a failure! You aren't a real entrepreneur unless you feel like this at least 600 times a week.

4 years into running my business and I still have those moments where I feel hopeless and doubtful, or like I'm running in place with everything I'm doing. I would always call my friends and loved ones and they'd talk me off the cliff I was on, but what really helped me was ME! Whenever I had a project I was trying to make work, and started doubting myself, before I'd spazz out, I'd just step back, take a deep breath, and talk myself through it. Not from freaking out, but with the actual project. Not to brag, well yes to brag, but I've come up with some of my best ideas that way. Patience is

definitely something I wasn't born with, but as an entrepreneur, you have to force yourself to be patient at times with many things. You have to be patient when it comes to the overall growth of your business and progress you are making, but also with yourself. Your business grows, and you grow right along with it. The person, who I was 4-5 years ago, before all of this, is not the same person dropping knowledge on you right now.

Goals, Goals, Goals

What would an entrepreneur be without having goals? Goal setting is one of the hallmarks of being an entrepreneur. Our goals are what drive us, what wake us up in the morning with a smile, or wake you up in the middle of the night in a cold sweat. The goals that you set as an entrepreneur encourage growth within your business, keep you focused, and keep you motivated. For me, I have a giant white board in my bed room next to my bed. My mind never sleeps. I constantly have dreams of ideas, projects, things I can do, new things I can do with my business! So I just hop up and write it down on the board and make sense of it all in the morning.

How do you set goals? Well you have to know what you want first! Yeah, yeah, we know you want to be successful, but what does success mean to you? Is success, being able to help 2 people a day, or 2 people a minute? The kind of goals that you set for yourself is incredibly important to your business' productivity and success. My rule for setting goals is to be realistic, be specific, and be ambitious.

Be realistic

- When you are setting goals for yourself, stop for a moment and think. "Am I really going to do this? Can I do this? Is this attainable?" In my opinion, anything is possible when you set your mind to it, but depending on where you are at with your business, some goals may not be realistic at that time, and only you can assess what that means for your business.

Be specific

- I go back to my previous point; you have to know what it is you want in order to work towards it. Don't be general in your goals, be specific that allows for a clear game plan to be made to achieve it. Don't just say, I want to increase profit. Okay...increase profits how? By how much? By when? You've got to be specific in what you want, how you want it, and when you want it by.

Be ambitious

- Entrepreneurship is a risky path to take for anyone, but never let that stop you from being ambitious in the future of your business. Like I said before, you can achieve anything you set your mind to. It's possible, but again you have to be willing to do what it takes to get it. Being realistic with yourself about your goals and your business' future, and being specific in that immediate or long term future, will allow you to be successful beyond your wildest dreams.

Do Your Research

So you want to start a business huh? Well good! Like I mentioned before I've always known that I wanted to start a business. Since I was in high school, I remember day dreaming while walking home from school of having a huge skyscraper in my town that had my name on it. My office was at the top floor of course, and I'd arrive and all my assistants and employees would rush to me to sign off on things, open doors for me, and pretty much worship me as I made my way to my office. Eventually I'd snap out of my day dream so that I didn't get hit by a car or anything for not paying attention because I was too busy in my own head.

Apart of what kept my mind going, and help my business become what it is today, is research. This is probably going to be one of the easiest and most fun things you do, and you'll constantly do this throughout your career. Now when I say research, I literally mean going to Google, or whatever search engine you prefer, and find out what you want to know. Be it, what's the best camera to use for photos on the beach, or what's the best computer software for website creation, or how to file your business taxes. There is no shame in asking questions, even dumb questions! How else are you going to know? Starting a business requires that you be open minded to a lot of things and perspectives. Never be to high on your horse, to Google something. I say Google because I was always glued to a computer so it was usually my first line of fire before finding someone to talk to. Make sure you are getting information from credible sources as well; I'd even recommend finding someone that you can take your questions to. Like if you are planning on starting a business in the PR industry, reach out to another PR company with your questions. Or if you want to know what you need to do to get your business license, reach out to another entrepreneur who may already have theirs. Research can be frustrating if you aren't getting the answers you may want, but keeping that open mind keeps your hopes up and helps in keeping you focused on your goals.

Research the competition

- Now I'm not telling you to go and sneak around outside of their establishment, or buy a disguise and pretend to be a customer of theirs...but wouldn't that be cool? Sounds like an episode of

Spongebob, haha. If you are starting a business within any industry, you need to know who your competition is. This is important to do because of course you want to know what you are going up against, and also you want to know what may be needed within the industry. For example, you may want to start a blanket business; well there may be only companies out there that sell red blankets and green blankets for $10 each at each place. **Sidebar:** I would also look at reviews of your competition in finding out what's lacking in the industry. All the companies out here now are selling and red and green blankets, so you may decide to sell red, green, and blue blankets for $5 each, and offer a free sandwich for those who buy all three as a treat. Take Chick-fil-a for instance, they sell chicken sandwiches and fries like many other fast food chains, but what's different about them? The experience. From the time you walk in, to the minute you walk out, they provide you with incredible customer service that you won't get anywhere else. The goal isn't to take down your competition, it's to not only give the customer options, but to give them what they are lacking elsewhere. Sounds kind of like an affair don't you think? You want the customer to fall and love with you and leave their wife, which in this case would be your competition.

- When doing this, you also want to make sure that you can actually supply your customers with their demands! You don't want to tell people that you offer a particular service that no one else in the area may offer, and not be very good at it or not be able to guarantee it to your customers. It can create a not so friendly reputation for yourself and your business.

Research your industry

- It's important to know what's the current state of the industry you are starting a business, even after you've started a business you want to know what's happening, that's include trends, the job market, everything! You can't be a successful business unless you are knowledgeable of your industry of course. For example, I don't think there were many people signing up to open their own real estate agency during the economic slump we were in a few years ago. But now the industry is booming and everyone is signing up to be a real estate agent!

Research your business

- Of course you should research your own business all the time once you've gotten started! I personally look for articles, reviews, comments, anything I can find because, good or bad, that's feedback that can help you. You want to know what people think of you and your business, your products, your customer service, you're everything. Personally, I am not ashamed to think that I can do no wrong. I'm awesome; I can't help but think that. So for me, looking at reviews, seeing what people are saying and thinking of my business helps me see things from the other side, and it helps you also understand how you are being received by the public. It's also good to search for businesses like yours and see if yours comes off, and if so, where does it fall. Is it the first to come up? The last? Second to last?

If you don't think your customers, or the general public, are receiving you correctly from what research you do on yourself, then that's your cue to go back to the drawing board and see what needs to be fixed.

Networking 101

Technology has truly spoiled people to the point that they are too lazy to meet people anymore. I mean, yeah sure, you can meet people and network online but there is nothing more worthwhile then good ole offline interactions and meetings. Our phones and computers may answer so many of life's questions, but unfortunately; meeting people still requires you to go out and actually MEET PEOPLE. Scary right? But don't cry, it's not as terrible as you may think.

I grew up a terribly shy person. Hard to believe right? I hate talking to people, hated social settings, and hated being in public in general. Starting my business for me was a huge step and I was well aware that I was going to half to put my fears to the side and go out into the world, but I tried and tried to find ways around it. I would make connections with people online and they'd want to meet with me in person to discuss a project or do an interview. I remember thinking sometimes, "gosh, why can't you just stay in the computer?"

But one day I just got tired of all of it and went to my first networking event! I was sweating like crazy, so nervous, didn't know what to do or what to say! But then, people started coming up to me and talking to me. They wanted to know about me, about my business, and as shocked as I was, I was actually able to hold real conversations with them without shaking uncontrollably or running out of the room. Years later, having worked through those issues, I see and understand now why and how it's so important to network and to actually talk about yourself and your business.

This new age of entrepreneurship now has created a breed of professionals that are accessible now. When you walk into an establishment, or call into a place, you can actually speak to or meet the owner. Because of this, people can ask the questions they wish they could ask people like Oprah and Bill Gates. What's the key to your success? What keeps your motivated? What makes your business so unique from others? Why did you start a business? What are you hoping to do for the community you serve? Networking is really a more causal form of sales. You are selling yourself and your business to other entrepreneurs, or professionals, who may be able to help your business.

Building connections and making friends is what help business thrive individually, and helps communities be as awesome as they are. I've been to numerous networking events over the years and I've learn some key things:

Always have an elevator pitch.

- When you are talking to someone at a function, where there are hundreds of other people there, you want to be able to introduce yourself and explain your business in as short, concise, and creatively as possible. Hence why it's called an elevator pitch, you have just as much time to catch and keep their attention, as you do on a quick elevator ride up a few stories. It's like you are dumbing down what your business is, but leaving a lasting impression at the same time.

Always get a business card, and always follow up

- I've made a number of connections at networking events that stared and ended there. But those connections you make don't have to end as soon as you walk back to your car, following up with a person is what makes a connection stick and creates a relationship. My technique is to give them my business card, and I take theirs as well or at least get their contact information, when I leave, I sit in my car and email all of those people I met asking to meet for lunch or coffee, really just an opportunity to see where this could go. If you don't get a response right away, wait a week and maybe follow up through another means. Like if you sent an email first, give them a call next, if no luck with the call, then wait a few days and send another email advising them that you're "interested in connecting again, whenever it's doable for them." See? Simple, easy, fair.

Be funny, or memorable

- The previous two tips will make your business memorable, but you want to also make sure that people remember you. You may not think you are much, but you want those people to leave there Googling your name and business to see who the heck you are, or chasing you down when you are walking out of the door. What works for me is telling jokes or coming up with funny stories, most of the time they are fake, to share with people on different things. You only have a few minutes to make an impact, might as well go out with a laugh!

<u>Sidebar:</u> Talk about your business all the time and to everyone. It will seem like you are being super annoying, but don't worry the feeling will pass. You never know what kind of connections you can make, and the only way you do that is by opening up. I remember once I was in the gas station looking for candy, and I was wearing a shirt that had my logo on it. The cashier started chatting me up about it, told her about my business, and how I was looking for someone to print t-shirts for my apparel, long story short, her boyfriend makes t-shirts and she gave me his number. Remember, your business is your child! Talk about it as much as you would if it were an actual kid!

Separate Business and Personal

There is a very weird complex about starting a business. You start a business because, PERSONALLY, that's what you want to do. You PERSONALLY want to follow your dreams, and PERSONALLY want to bring about change in your life, community, and the world. Starting a business is a PERSONAL decision, to take time out of your PERSONAL life to do. But once you've started that business, it's important that you draw a line between business and personal. Seems like a contradiction with everything I just said right? Don't worry, I'm making my point.

I like to compare starting a business, to having a child. Once you've given birth to that idea, it becomes its own being. It's living and breathing, and everything that you do from that point on is detrimental to it staying alive. Drawing the line between business and personal is really more about you than the business. It allows for there to be clear organization in your life on both sides especially when it comes to time management, prioritizing things, and relationships. This is probably going to be one of the hardest things that you do, mainly because separating business from personal has to be done on a number of different levels.

Friendships and Relationships

I'm going to say this once, and I'll continue to stand by this: Doing business with people who started out as your friend, never works. I know what you are thinking, "well Kim, if they are your friends, they should support what you do. You should be able to trust them with anything." I'm sure there are some friends that may be exempt to this, but it's important to understand that not ALL of your friends are good people to do business with. Perfect example: I had a friend, let's call her...STUPID. So STUPID and I were friends for a while and she was such a supporter of what I was doing. She'd always brag on me and what I was working on, I could talk to her about things that were happening, like she was a real friend.

One day, STUPID decided that she wanted to join my team and help with projects I was working on and various other things. Going into this, I thought, what could go wrong? EVERYTHING WENT WRONG. I would assign her certain tasks and give her a deadline; she'd never complete them when I needed them. I think friends think that, they don't have to conduct themselves a different way or actually listen to you because you guys are friends! So they think if they don't meet a deadline that it's fine because we are friends! If they don't show up for something, it's fine because we are friends! I thought that because she was my friend and she knew how serious I was about my business, knew how passionate I was about this that that would be more reason for her to take it seriously also. What's even more insane is that, once I started getting really fed up of her excuses and slack, I tried talking it out with her and she said, "Well, I'll just take my percentage of the company and we can end this now." She actually thought after months of doing less than the bare minimum that she was entitled to something at the end! The only percentage she had, was 100% of a fist in the face at this point. Let's just say we are friends anymore.

Now, that's not to say that you can't be friends with anyone when you are an entrepreneur because you can! I've met some incredible people who have become some of my best friends since owning my business. I've worked with them professionally and we can party on the weekends together. The point of my story is to say, some friends, should just stay friends. Just because STUPID was a good friend to me, doesn't mean that she was going to make a good employee and teammate. I'm sure if I never brought her on to my team, maybe our friendship would have last longer. Well...maybe not, she was kind of a bitch. But anyway! So before you make your friend a business partner, employee, or teammate, make your position as an entrepreneur clear to them. You as a friend and you as an entrepreneur have to be two different people, and show them that, it could possibly even make your friendship stronger. Don't tolerate behavior that could potential hurt your business or reputation either!

Money

Many people who first start out their businesses, still work full time job, or at least have a household they need to provide for. One of the awesome things about having a business is that, you'll make money, and then sometimes you won't. Either way, it's important to separate those funds from and for the business, away from personal funds and income. For example, I still work a full time job now, even with my business growing as much as it is. I still have bills, household expenses, etc. that I have to pay, that I use my money from my full time job to pay for. Meanwhile, I still have money, although it may not be a lot, coming in regularly from my business. Remember when I told you that running a business was like having a child? Well guess what, that child is going to need things ALL THE TIME. When I first got started, I needed equipment, I need to purchase a domain for my website, and I needed materials. Me, being the bright eyed and bushy tailed entrepreneur I was, I took my whole paycheck and bought everything I needed. Now that was awesome for my business, but on the flip side, in my personal life, I struggled. Because I had dumped my funds in to my business so fast, and didn't have a plan to cover my personal expenses and bills, I basically shot myself in the foot financially. Well, for at least the next two weeks.

    It's okay to pace yourself financially, and in the beginning you'll have to. You don't have to buy the most expensive computer right away; you can start off with the cheap one and then save up for the expensive one. I know you're probably stomping your feet and pouting but hey, if you want to break your pockets right away then be my guest! It's better to start off small and then grow from there. Always keep in mind; Steve Jobs started Apple in his garage!

Pacing yourself and budgeting are great things to do no matter what phase you are in with your business, and a stress free way of doing that is by separating your monies early on. Best way to do that is by having your personal bank account, and a separate business banking account as well. I preferably think it's best to have them both at the same institutions, so that if you ever have money you want to transfer in between accounts it's easier, and creates a paper trail. It's also good to set it up that way if you ever decide to apply for a business loan or you are filing your taxes, you can prove what kind of money you have coming in and going out of your business. You'll also have debit cards for both, so if you are shopping for the business, you can use the business card, if you are shopping for yourself, use the personal card.

Another thing that I like about it is that you can keep track of your spending habits and make adjustments as needed. Like, if you run a business that requires you to do a lot of printing and you're constantly going to Staples to print things that can really add up. You could compare how much you are spending on printing, to how much it would be to purchase your own printer, and maybe cut those costs and save money. See? It's all about growth!

Trust me; running your business off of your personal account is more of headache than you think.

So it's better to separate the two early on, to make life a lot easier, especially as your business grows. Saving receipts is also a good thing too! When you file your taxes, you can write all of those things off and probably get a pretty penny back as well.

Teach Yo Self

I remember my first few months as an entrepreneur. I had absolutely no clue what I was doing. I would go on social media and look for people who had successful businesses of their own, and ask for guidance and help. I kept getting the door shut in my face, no response or help, or I'd have to pay them in order to get them to help me do anything. I know I mentioned before that you should definitely reach out to people when researching your industry and competition. One of the unfortunate side effects of entrepreneurship for many people is an inflated ego. There are some really, really mean people who own businesses that don't want to help, they don't want to talk, they don't want you to own a business either so they will make your interactions with them as unpleasant as possible to discourage you, make you angry, and make you give up. DON'T LET THEM. The shortcomings of others don't have to be the end all be all for you and your dream. One unpleasant encounter is just that. ONE. They are going to happen, they are going to disappoint you, but don't let it distract you, let it encourage you. Your passion for what you do will be tested, CONSTANTLY, be familiar with it, but also be above it.

Whenever I'd encounter people like the ones I just mentioned, they would just make me feel so bad! I'd question everything like, "OMG what am I doing? I can't do this! I don't know how to do this!" But after being let down so many times, I just stopped reaching out to people. While in the midst of doing research on evening for my business, I went on YouTube and found a crap load of tutorial videos on how to do EVERYTHING. I taught myself how to use a camera, edit videos, do graphics, how to do particular things on social media, everything I wanted to learn from others I taught myself in a matter of a few days. If you aren't getting the help you need, don't be afraid to learn for yourself. It's one of the most rewarding parts of about being an entrepreneur, the chance to learn and experience new things. So don't let people's lack of enthusiasm to help you stop your growth, learn for yourself and grow even more.

CEO vs. Entrepreneur

Let's just got ahead and clear the air right now. A CEO and an entrepreneur are two different things. Let me say it one more time for the people in the back... A CEO AND AN ENTREPRENEUR ARE TWO DIFFERENT THINGS. It's so weird to me how people start a business and already start calling themselves the CEO. "Oh I'm the CEO of blah blah blah!" Before you rush and add CEO to your email signature, it is very important to understand the difference for yourself and for the business.

CEO stands for Chief Executive Officer, which is the highest-ranking executive manager in an organization. An entrepreneur is a person that starts a business. Both are important roles in a company and both are decision makers within a business. Now when you look at both of these definitions, it's clear that the entrepreneur is the owner, and the CEO is just a top manager. But just because the owner is essential higher than the CEO, doesn't mean that the CEO may have to answer to an owner.

Sometimes the owner may not be in the picture at all, which puts the CEO ultimately in charge. In some organizations, an owner may have nothing to do with the day-to-day operations of the company, and only make decisions regarding big picture things for the company. There is really no mandatory format to the leadership hierarchy, but ultimately that's decided by the entrepreneur, because the business does not exist without them! For example, if you started a business and decided you wanted someone else to actually run the business, or manage it, you could do that! Or if you wanted to start the business, and give it to someone else, you can do that as well! When you take that risk of starting a business, it's important that you understand what YOU want to do, and what type of role you want to have within this business. Starting a business is essentially the easy part, but do you have what it takes to actually run a business?

    Establishing that leadership hierarchy is also important if you are going into business with multiple people. I remember once I went to interview this local record label, and when I asked the three members to introduce themselves, they each called themselves some variation of CEO. It was confusing and you could tell there was some tension when each person stated their title, and trust, I could not stop laughing when I left. I laughed because it was clear they had never had a conversation on whose role was what or at least who is in charge, and the obvious awkward tension that came proved why it is so important to establish that from the beginning to hopefully prevent conflict and add structure to the business.

    Now not every business is going to need a CEO, or a President, or a manager. You, as the entrepreneur, may be the only employee and that's fine. Or you may want to run things in the beginning and once the business grows to a certain point, then you may bring in a CEO or a manager, or other roles that will be important in making your business stronger. My favorite piece of advice to any entrepreneur is that, what make work for A, may not work for B. Just because Amber may be running her business perfectly as the owner, and has a CEO that handles the day to day operations for her, doesn't mean that YOU need to have a CEO as well. It may be necessary for Amber to do that depending on what industry she is in, what kind of business she has, how far in her business she is, and the kind of role that she herself chooses to have within the organization.

Fail Your Heart Out

Failing is something that you will be amazing at when you are an entrepreneur. Well, I'm sure you are good at other things, but failing is definitely going to be added to the list. And sometimes, you don't even really fail, you may feel like you are failing or like a failure because you may not be making the progress you want to me, or something did go the way that you planned for it to go so you're stuck with this feeling. I personally hate that feeling but I love failing, not that I do it intentionally. Failures are hidden opportunities for you to win again. People make the mistake of being focused on how the failure made them feel, and not on what it made them learn or think.

One of my favorite quotes comes from one of the greatest movies, based on the backstory of THE GREATEST superhero ever, and that is Batman. In Batman Begins, after Bruce's house is burned down, he and Alfred make their way to the Batcave and Alfred asks him, "Why do we fall?" to which Alfred responds, "To learn how to pick ourselves back up."

Think of failures as conditioning for successes, so that you can learn how to appreciate them and handle them. Ever thought about that? Can you actually handle success? All successful people fail; it's the reason why they are so successful. You learn some of your biggest lessons when you are down, but even when you fail it's important to get back up and reflect on what happen. What could I have done differently? Did I do anything right? Hard questions to ask but the answers will humble you.

Be Your Own Cheerleader

I'm sorry to do this to you again but...I have bad news. You are NOT always going to have the support everyone when running a business. Accepting this is one of the most heartbreaking things about being an entrepreneur. Oh my god you started a business!

Whoo! This is a big step in your life! Whoo! Sometimes, this is about as much support that you'll get from people when you are just starting out. I can recall when I first started, a lot of people thought I was dumb to do something like this. They didn't see an "immediate profit," from the dream that I had, and because of that, they made sure not to support me in any way. Even when I would host events and promote them on social media, tell everyone about it, I'd expect a packed house but end up with the place being emptier than it is before it opens. I was hurt, I felt defeated and alone because I felt like no one cared about what I was trying to do, no one cared about how important this was to me.

    It took me quite a while to realize it but you know who the only supporter you need is? YOU. Also long as you support your business, and your efforts, everyone else doesn't matter. Like I mentioned before, you have to be self-motivated enough to stick it out when you are the last one standing. The support will come, but it won't if you give up before it comes to you. But until then, understand that you don't need others validation, or seal of approval, in order for your business to be a success. Think of it like being single, you have to love yourself in order for someone else to love you. If you support your business and stand behind what it is and is all about, people will see that, resonate with it, and the support will come. OH! I thought of another metaphor! Remember Noah from the bible, and remember when God told him, "build the arc, and they will come." That's essentially the same thing here. Build the foundation, and the support will come. Give them something to support, not just because its just you, but give them something to actually support, and it will come.

Wait At Your Own Risk

I have never been a very...patient person. I tend to have a habit of rushing into things sometimes, or being too exciting to take the next step when doing something. I think when patience was being passed out; I stepped out to go to the bathroom. So yes, I'm a proud impatient person. This is a blessing and curse, but we will focus on the blessing side of it for right now.

When we are kids we have such wild imaginations and create these big plans for ourselves, but there is always someone that says, "Oh, when you're older you can do that!" So we wait...and wait...and wait...and then we get older, and we're still told we have to wait to do things. "Oh, you can't do that right now! You should wait a while." How much longer do I have to wait to do what I desire to do? You've clearly taken advantage of an opportunity in your life to start a business, or even thinking of starting one, so why should you have to continue to wait? If you have an idea, if you have something you want to do, DO IT! Of course, you want to make sure you have a plan in place to execute this and ensure it will go well, but still, don't wait! It may not go well the first time, but every failure is an opportunity for you to learn and improve. Nothing gets done when you are just waiting, or you make excuses for why you can't take your business to the next level or why you can't add a new service or product to your business. Don't doubt yourself; give yourself a chance to do something. We're not kids anymore; we don't have to wait on the future anymore!

    I have a client of mines that is in the early stages of starting a business. She has the name, concept, plan, and everything in place, but she doesn't have her mobile app for the business up and running yet. She's constantly going to networking events, meeting people, and talking about the business, but she's not being active with the actual business. So essentially, she's talking about a business she isn't doing anything with. Every time we talk she says, "Well, I don't know, I think we should wait a while..." and when I ask how long a while is she doesn't give me a very clear answer. I say that to say this,

Always Reflect

Every time I achieve something, or meet a goal, I go back to my drawing board and reflect on how I got here, and how I can get even further. Reflecting on what you have done and what you are doing helps you to see things from another angle. Take stock in what's working for you and what's not working. Make a list of those things and think about how you can make those things that aren't working for you actually work, or how you can replace them with things that can work. Sometimes when reflecting, it's good to have someone else help you do this. I always bring one of my close friends in because they see the things that you don't see, add those to the list as well.

Once you've done that, look at your goals. Are you on the right track to meet those goals? Have you met any already? Do you need to change any of them? Once you've looked at your goals, I always encourage people to think about where you wanna be in 6 months, think about where you wanna be in 2 years, and think about where you wanna be in 5 years. Align those with the goals you already have, make adjustments, think on them, and then get to work! It's important to constantly take time to reassess and make sure your house is in order, because sometimes we lose track or may fall down, so we have to take a moment to remind ourselves of where we are headed in order to refocus and get back to work!

Sidebar: Do yourself a favor and invest in a notebook, a marker board, and a big calendar. These will be your whole world, and not only help you stay organized, but also help you get your thoughts in order. I use my marker board the most, especially when brainstorming, making to-do lists, planning events, just everything.

Conclusion

Round of applause for you! Whoo! You read the whole book and now have the tools and advice you need to wage war on the world with your dreams and ideas. Entrepreneurship is truly one of the world's greatest inventions and the most rewarding experience a person could have. Well...besides having kids...or getting married...but whatever. Being able to think of something and to bring it to life was an incredible feeling for me when I started my business. Do me a favor, one day while you are diligently working on things, just stop and look at what you are doing. Look at what you've accomplished and created for just a moment. Feels good doesn't it? Feels good to be able to say to yourself, or tell people, "I did that!" It won't be perfect, and it doesn't have to be, but it's yours. It's all of your hard work, late nights, blood, sweat, and tears, YOUR DREAM, manifested into your business.

Recap!

Business Name _____

The Structure of my Business is...

_____

☐ Articles of Organization/Incorporation or Certificate of LP/LLP filed?

☐ Operating Agreement/Bylaws or Resolutions/LP or LLP Agreement filed?

My EIN Number is

_____

☐ Trademarked your logo/business name?

☐ Copyrighted product?

☐ Business License?

☐ Other permits needed?

_____

Create 10 Goals for the Month

Remember: Be Realistic, Be Specific, Be Ambitious!

1)

2)

3)

4)

5)

6)

7)

8)

9)

10)

Create 10 Goals for the Month

Remember: Be Realistic, Be Specific, Be Ambitious!

1)

2)

3)

4)

5)

6)

7)

8)

9)

10)

Create 10 Goals for the Month

Remember: Be Realistic, Be Specific, Be Ambitious!

1)

2)

3)

4)

5)

6)

7)

8)

9)

10)

Create 10 Goals for the Month

Remember: Be Realistic, Be Specific, Be Ambitious!

1)

2)

3)

4)

5)

6)

7)

8)

9)

10)

Create 10 Goals for the Month

Remember: Be Realistic, Be Specific, Be Ambitious!

1)

2)

3)

4)

5)

6)

7)

8)

9)

10)

Create 10 Goals for the Month

Remember: Be Realistic, Be Specific, Be Ambitious!

1)

2)

3)

4)

5)

6)

7)

8)

9)

10)

Create 10 Goals for the Month

Remember: Be Realistic, Be Specific, Be Ambitious!

1)

2)

3)

4)

5)

6)

7)

8)

9)

10)

Create 10 Goals for the Month

Remember: Be Realistic, Be Specific, Be Ambitious!

1)

2)

3)

4)

5)

6)

7)

8)

9)

10)

Create 10 Goals for the Month

Remember: Be Realistic, Be Specific, Be Ambitious!

1)

2)

3)

4)

5)

6)

7)

8)

9)

10)

Create 10 Goals for the Month

Remember: Be Realistic, Be Specific, Be Ambitious!

1)

2)

3)

4)

5)

6)

7)

8)

9)

10)

Create 10 Goals for the Month

Remember: Be Realistic, Be Specific, Be Ambitious!

1)

2)

3)

4)

5)

6)

7)

8)

9)

10)

Create 10 Goals for the Month

Remember: Be Realistic, Be Specific, Be Ambitious!

1)

2)

3)

4)

5)

6)

7)

8)

9)

10

www.ingramcontent.com/pod-product-compliance
Lightning Source LLC
Chambersburg PA
CBHW050016230526
45470CB00003B/991